as far as I can see

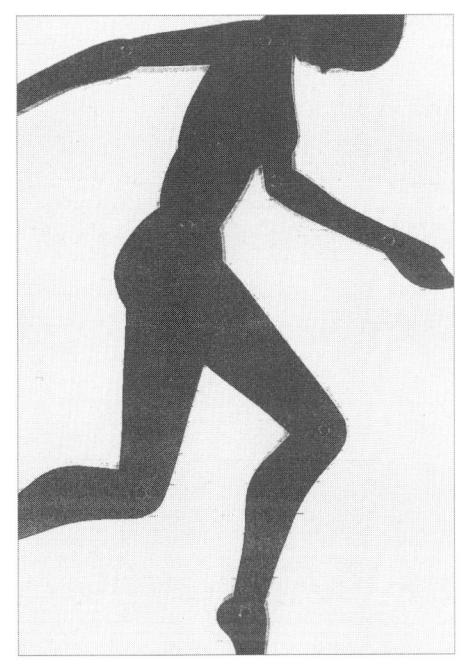

ALSO BY MICHELE LEGGOTT

Like This? (1988)
Reading Zukofsky's 80 Flowers (1989)
Swimmers, Dancers (1991)
Dia (1994)

EDITOR

Opening the Book (1995, with Mark Williams)
The Victory Hymn by Robin Hyde (1995)
The Book of Nadath by Robin Hyde (1999)

as far as I can see

Michele Leggott

AUCKLAND UNIVERSITY PRESS

ACKNOWLEDGEMENTS

I wish to thank Rona Dyer for permission to reproduce 'Girl Bathing' from her *Engravings on Wood* (Caxton, 1948) and a detail of a later print from the same block.

Earlier versions of some of these poems appear at http://wings.buffalo.edu/epc/authors/leggott and in Sally Rodwell's film *Heaven's Cloudy Smile*. Magazine publication includes *A Brief Description of the Whole World* (Auckland), *The Capilano Review* (Vancouver), *JAAM* (Wellington), *Jacket* (http://www.jacket.zip.com.au), *The Pander* (Auckland), *Salt* (Fremantle), *Sulfur* (Ypsilanti, Mich.) and *Trout* (http://www.auckland.ac.nz/lbr/trout).

Sampling from the poems of Robin Hyde in the Iris Wilkinson Papers at the University of Auckland Manuscripts & Archives Collection: AU 97/1 37.1, 101.1, 102.1, 112.1, 242.1, 275, 397.1, 400.1, 402.2, 443.1, 470.1, 601, 604, 610.

First published 1999

Auckland University Press
University of Auckland
Private Bag 92019
Auckland
New Zealand
www.auckland.ac.nz/aup

© Michele Leggott 1999

ISBN 1 86940 217 0

Publication is kindly assisted by
ARTS COUNCIL OF NEW ZEALAND *TOI AOTEAROA*

Cover images from *Heaven's Cloudy Smile*, 1998. (Sally Rodwell, director; Alan Brunton, Sally Rodwell & Michele Leggott, script; Richard Bluck, cinematography). Used by permission.
© 1998 Red Mole/Glenis Giles Films, PO Box 7356, Wellington South.

Cover design by Christine Hansen
Printed by Publishing Press Ltd, Auckland

contents

fortunes

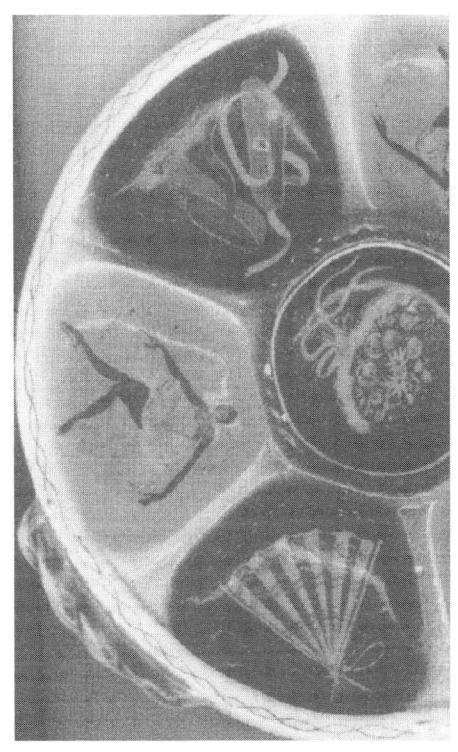

beatrix.song

I am a dream best left to the ache

and space of letters virtual

upon a screen   look where I stand

in the heart's domain demesne *demain*

à joual we'll spin together on the thermals

given out across the breathing of that season

made sheer by the body's load   who lives

does loves writes I have your promise

beating residues and tricks of light   look

where I stood against the grey morning

and watched you sleep   now wake

be about the spirals you describe for me

the letters never better left than to the ache

and treacheries of dream   yes wake

thoroughfares await them

between city and heaven dear bird a coin

for eyes for the animal thrown onto the road

tattered drum dazzled cones *that we may abolish*

disaster the stars lean down inviolate aspects

and touch the world at twenty four points

to read its upturned face   *Heal with a star*

her eyes it said and loss spread out

a dozen blankets against the purple wind

but still we couldn't shake malfeasance   o bird

happy in fluent grass how will you make

the starry marches and silk of the sky

tumble yard by yard

into the lap of a woman spinning

thin dreams from perfect other places

crying

his hall's flown into his bird heavy weather

on the neural highway but we know

what he means he means anima

heaven's daughter in the rafters panicking

and incommensurate   I didn't see it

nor wings nor crown but heard the stony spaces ring

one winter morning walking by and that was not

divagation but all instances of bird and ceilings

rolled to one particular to me to you two dollar song

what can I hope for to break us out of error

so that the words fly up and the walls do not fall

a bird in the cloisters the sudden downpour

drench of memory warmly losing and abusing

confusing sense and *Benedict's neighbour* alike

in winter

she was playing in a meadow I could not see

and fell miraculously past jeopardy and speech

everything was lost   we stepped off the railway

into an extension of the great landscape preparing

to forget our existence   the world was nothing

but planes and mirrors that link and space

the sugars of its invention   of meat and drink

at that dark table she took not and now like the rose

dances with all her body because the little seeds

have not been found   *destructive dove* or

fearful one walking in the gardens of the dead

when you pick the red fruit breathless risk

darts in at the gate again   swallow swallow

the stories black about you in the rainy air

limen amabile

it is the hurt place *lapis by jade*

to which none returns unharmed *vermeil*

by turquoise bit beloved pitiless city of light

I have come asking the price of the heart broken

will you restore her into my arms   *lost contours*

round-expressed feast of trumpets feast of lights

festivals of lucid vigil a feather's weight collapses

for love clair-audient on the doorstep   *Lords*

of the whole mosaic fervent industrials *how you fit*

gem into gem but cannot find the breather who is

everywhere and gone   I see *what's strange to you*

transformation's gift taking place before my eyes

she holds a snake a white stick she gives

into my hand and I go tapping into the world

dove

persephatta

swimming in the black river a tale emerges

twists and turns about her sometimes urgent

sometimes mirror blank   she doesn't play

lazy riverine though the water lip laps

surfaces and resumes such talk along her flanks

that strength runs out as need walks in

riparian parties onto the wintery tombolo

river I put my trust in plum blossom words

dragged under leaving no language safe

from itself   a girl going to meet her mother

is abducted marries death fixes destruction

in her own image   the script has lashed her

to sufficiency and reticence those broken limbs

in the current she steps from wholly diffident

persicifolia

and with rescues to effect   *peachleaved nymph*

sorrowing (are you sorrowing?) on the waters

bearing you to heaven's presumptuous grin

mock pursuits and marriage beds collapse the letter

space where a diction hides her people   bride fly out

of his hand who wades the Money Pool at sunset

and stumbles across the aporia at dawn singing

heaven is here in a kiss   gifts of prophecy and healing

pucker the valley of that leaf you copied

to the body in perpetuity   your mouth is leaves

on his face   nymphæ   peachleaf   bride

of loops and costume change swirling cerulean

in the stream a blue lotus a white lotus vanishing

bride   peachleaf   nymphæ   your mouth leaves

9

persica

his face a court of angels upriver

twelve dynasties east and drumming the morning star

into the arms of the sun   your *ha* is an almond in flower

above the heart that hears his *hu* and is unbound

uproarious with æons going past in a shout

a shimmy on the grape ropes a ripple up the pool

beholder to beggar to pleader please

walk with me here in the spring   there is no foot

can be imagined without its wing no convention

without the literal honey the literal where

and when and how the literal sleeps as on a body

of water solely its coeval estimate of drift

Angelike   *where* twelve twelves with wings

upraise another hungry drummer of spring

persienne

ah persienne   the wind takes my breath away

I see it over the blue islands laughing like six children

looking out to sea   their voices rise higher and higher

their mountain is the bellied sail taking them now

to meet everything that was wished   in the printed folds

rivers of air gardens of wind and the sea-going craft

drawn up near the place they have called Paradise

ah persienne   breathless they reassign what is given

I was asleep dreaming in a dark place   it pressed

on me and I was afraid   the weeping dove was lost

to the sea roads the air gardens had forgotten her

deft play about the topsails   it is recalled

by the high voices in their eagerness to be

embarked *this dear morning* into the outward

perse

spray of blossom whiter than oceans

jumping together over the reef run wild

into the sea   *I go to libraries*

because they are the ocean the spray of blossom

she is bending passion *a wavecrest* mountaineer

of the word and the body which reads *Everest*

floating like that like a summer's night resolved

a glitter in the long hazy dawn   and dove

among the waves at last herself morning

and evening star but one body *I   not my eyes*

reading day in day out the little distance

carried forward by the jacaranda in bloom

over the gate and the foot jubilant in kicking

its elemental doubts into the sky *per se*

h e s p e r i d e s

Lima dolce 1699

In Hrn: Doct: Silberrad garten.

dolce

oranges seem to grow wild in the bay that is *cloud*

carried by the wind   there my boys swim out

of the easterly blow *Haukapua* they shout

the huff and the hook the kick and the splash

the green bay is full of their golden bodies   persistent

ungentle the wind rides overhead as they trail back

for showers by the open window a towel on the pillow

sweet rhythms of the bach where they wake and sleep

to arithmetical Variations on shelter and a doorway

the performance of the sun at noon a memory printing

windmills under the canopy of leaves   *highly aromatic*

days of no event but virtuoso growth how tall

they are how straight of limb what storms of noise

the keyboards take to be sure the game proceeds

getting away

angel wings beating harder than ever light drumming

on skinny shoulders pertinent to select displays of

temper and charm   it was always important to knock

with your elbow a dozen beer smoked kahawai something

to put on the table   then to wear as little as possible

as long as possible to eat late sleep lots and sit around

talking in the dark remembering *the buzzing of the bees*

in the lemonade trees looking over at Paku so built up

big rock candy mountain on its estuary of song

hurricane surf that had to be swum hand in hand

under skies blue enough to discreate a cyclone

there is white sand mile after mile in loneliness

and crushed shells giving it a border of violet

we stop later for the golden oysters of Miranda

a nautilus

I put the children to bed and go out

hunting the ancestors   the one who is afraid

of the night adrift up there in his deep blue covers

the one who will curl between us so quietly

nobody wakes and he is safe   I have left them again

unable to sleep and knowing their sleeping

is my return *to the wide nets washing out in moonlight*

they stir as the house gears down they call out

as I pass I call back I am there when they stagger about

to gulp water and pee   they lock the doors I left open

and skim up ladders in their sleep   I need them

they prevent my disappearance from the world

they bring me back howling overacting for my blurred

attention the cradle boat drawn out on the falling tide

staying put

the girl on the fridge found her walled-up skin

but won't be without her magnetic babes   they frolic

around her a sea of alphabetic cries AzGVw sLK∃

yY hSPr fL0Op low on the feminine with a modicum

of consonantal drift *you get the picture* we get

the picture thrown around and stuck back *baby baby*

my sINGER Flips her fishy tail   *Mistakes I know*

I've made a few the impossible back-arch her attempts

at keeping it all up in the air *Citrus limetia* rare and interesting

though worthless a horticultural curiosity   which version

do you want three commas and a dash or four ellipses

following a special form of berry yes a *hesperidium*

what could be kept separate was never worth the bother

only human now she flippers every little morph

dulce

the Nuyoricans went to Piano Beach and found tai tane

unbelievably gentle   the messages were adjuncts

to their honeymoon performed in blacksand with a bag

of hot plums and a modesty of towels   we clapped

the lipsticks untwirling on the front veranda at home

we waited for the remembered fragrance and we listened

for the old motors overhead in the long light evening

candy I call my sugar candy and the letters he wrote her

persist with orangeblossom snipped from the ivory lace

of her panniers   *don't forget to change your flying boots*

she wrote him on the invitation thinking maybe

of this frangipani coming into flower on the porch

most admired veranda and of the hesper ride

his DC 3 still charters for our collaborating hearts

torches

song

twenty three and a half

degrees unstoppered

in the night garden to which

your lips are scripture

and ecliptic tilt in one

flamboyant kiss   curse

her who with half a head

twenty three and a half

degrees celestial sought

among these one moment

in arrest forgetting the stop

put to the garden

as it bumped us and time

stood entreatied in your face

dark torch

hey old flame   I swam

across the harbour just to buy you

some shoes   all night all night

in the water howling songs

uncontained publications of love

with a flea in its ear and its pants

on fire   fool! liar!

(waves arms) who am I to hold

a dark torch up to heaven

and the ferry's disappearing lights

I didn't have the boat fare

but I knew the fit of your feet

and the extraordinary hours kept

in that boutique   I swim aflame

one

sunny thankyou for the

billowing parachute

silk April wave

April morning winning

the fit of the hand

to the falls the sonnets

the lips retouched

the shell I am holding

sunny one so blue

in this place between

conquering surfaces

each word I flew

was its vanishing point

out on the alba sea

22

walking on air

two good ones

rolling over and over

one so loving

the other they change

places alternate

days turning the sky

cap of darkness

cap of daylight starry

retinue of sparrows

answering the sailors'

prayer Dioscuri

boys infrangible

gems how

is a bird's wing?

what is

it might be very early

it might be very late

fleecy marble the world

curve sticks out of

love's proper sphere

at the feet of the rider

stolen away for love

smoke touches the square

of the winged horse

and the lightfield explodes

blue flame and white

one handstand

for love stolen away

from the sooty altars

snake & jewel

learning

when will we live like that again?

first there was a city with its moons and cars

lawless comets and such discontinuous delight

that even going for a walk around the galaxy

was icecream in the park, sweet momentum

like a scattering of stars arriving to read

the book of tears to a crowd expecting opera

what next but the caduceus, dazed

imperatives wrapped about a talking stick

face to face and turn by turn reared back

to flap the wings of vision overhead   after this

the lily with its open mouth and ribbon spathes

bumpy erogeny bespeaking

the immaculate shape of things to come

helix

what can you give me that begins with *hinna?*

a vision twisting and twisting torch flame or genetic

material from the island of the first morning

a tenderness taking the lyric and turning it inside

out because nothing will ever be the same

a tantrum in the real house of days because some

of them must be picked up and lived despite

a vicissitude oh vicissitudes devouring

the delicate provender of body and soul

a patience on the ladder two steps short

of the full house each keeps for the other

a bed where text is getting around to being

what they want to do today   helix a rich tissue

helix her helix her helix her helix

lebh

and she's elixial elixirate a mystical etymology

suffused in his arms he drinks her she is

the fruit of the tree the river channel he swam

to get where he was going precious body

spread out along its honeysuckle paths *deep bloom*

being deep bloom being the names of his limbs

not *as* but *here* she touches him remembering

the words the wounds the double breath

the commotion not *here* but *now* his heart opens

precious fruit of the body shaking the tree

soluble drum on paths where she jumps too

Shekhinah bright heart reversing annihilation

jewel daughter song daughter light daughter

be laughter be stings be spoken be loud

hyle

the daughters of light, what are their qualities?

I come home from work and there's dinner to fix

I get into bed and it's swing down low *goodnight*

good morning waking up with you and the story

of my luminous being is lying on the floor

with the rest of the clothes I took off, hidden phases

of the mama I am and you want

to be on top of before the old and holy men ask

how it is the ever-queen distributes sugar grains

to the righteous then makes them clean their teeth

and block the sun with creams before they leave

for school   this you face *sweet poet* we cannot fall

asleep or in love until you see me through

the unsapphirine unsilvered mirror of where I am

all

out the window on damp wings heady scent

of lilies melisma's little kiss on the dark side

of whatever I was in the barefoot prayer flying over

overflying flown over overflowing coherence

one about the other history and desire objectively

perfect in a temple of particulars am*ple roma*n fleuve

a river novel on the full and just about to close

distances considered immanent but never audible

see we open at a page of choice the stars are out

the words are pure wonder   hys*sop hia*tus

we breathe calyp*so phia*ls and there's no trouble

distinguishing works and days   we speak

the ties then let them go flying in the places

where love was made and darkness held it close

oes & spangs

wild

orchids

this long talk
with desire
this long talk

detail which is the
mirage of seeing
detail which is

whisper now
what I will be
Whisper Now

a sleeping lover
in the poem's words
a sleeping lover

hoping the miracle
would happen
the miracle boat

honey in the throat
and singing
honey in the throat

carrying sounds
for the mirage and
sounds carrying

a light kiss a dark kiss
to be in love
a light kiss

I dug right in I went
everywhere I was
everywhere I was

and loved
in the third stanza
that stanza

I didn't need eyes
for that little pot
I didn't need eyes

which is a detail
a canopy a sleep
a sloop a sleep

the horses of lu
thundering la la
thundering

where do they come from
where do they go
they come & they go

32

look I will be Fishgirl
bouncing on a wave
Fishgirl bouncing

to the deep rolling around
on my tongue
deep rolling tongue

singing bare tits bare ass
long black hair
bare ass long hair

excursions diversions
consignments
diversions

to the waterline
mama you
the wave-line

eight minutes late
for the ball not counting
and counting

the mirror world the house
of days the big event
mirror world

so nice by the fire
in a Fish Cup
so nice

dust and foam
for another body
foam & dust

no bounce no song
no bare ass without you
without you

splashing in the tigerskin
behind the wave
tigerskin behind

in the cool and rainy months
fish with kick
in the cool months

oes and spangs
for the allegory this froth
oes & spangs

in my comb *honey*
you hot chocolate
honey comb

33

a woman, a rose, and what has it to do with her
or they with one another?

1

Do you see me? I am falling out of a blue sky where my days were
as dancers in a maze, sure-footed and smiling. I stood in my
garden pulling loquats off the tree and eating them to be full of
spring. I filled up on summer and kept the city busy with
correspondence. Flightpaths criss-crossed at my feet, bees fizzed
and joy was my middle name.

Then a pair of taxis went head to head in a distant country so
suddenly I didn't see the difference but it was a wide white
threshold. When I couldn't thread a needle, when I could no
longer see the faces of my children or trim their nails, when the
colour of money disappeared (and I bareheaded in the midday
sun) then falling began and I cried out against it. What's one wing
beating time on the steel drum of the sky? What is the sight of my
eyes to the great oratory of the labyrinth?

There was a send-off, they gave me flowers and asked where I
would go. To open the eyes of the soul, I said. Good wishes
hovered over the gathering and messages flew into my pockets.
There is a way, I said, but this is only the first gate. I give what is
left of the light of my eyes, I have fallen out of a clear sky.

2

How will you know me? My signs were set in heaven but they are lost. If I was ever the moon's daughter that name is gone too. I am the daughter of the widow's son, eldest daughter of an eldest son, eldest child of an eldest child. I am the daughter of the widow's child, eldest child of an only daughter, eldest daughter of the youngest child. Eldest son and youngest daughter, eldest and youngest of the widow women before and after the war, married on the first day of spring in a small mountain town.

The children built a house on the mountain. The children built a house by the sea. Their children were born and played there, they could tell you about the lino patterns or the plates driven around the kitchen at speed. They cooked salt dough in the stove on the bank and pulled out real fragrance for history. They remember hurt skin around the mouth stuck with blue gum that wouldn't come off. See them laugh, see them play. See Sweetie run.

But the widows' children died and were at last a white sift on the air of a mountain gully. I told their stories to my children, I made them live in the eyes of my sons, I watched the stories grow up by other shorelines, below other mountains.

I am not a daughter now and I cannot see my sons though I know they see me. This is the gate of tears, another farewell. Beyond it an aqueous humour prevails and we may swim, but not as once on a morning by the raft in a sea of flowers. Here I give up my dear ones.

3

What did you learn? Swoops sweeps swerves, I came along the waterfront at noon and saw everything in the arms of its other. A coin spun in the bright air. Six bow arms lifted by the fountain in the square, six bows flashing the noise of water, traffic and a stepping out in time for the dark crossing. All weathers are promised at the iris gate.

I, a pupil, a taut aperture and nimble, distinguishing abundance in the field from a chaos in the world, I set up a light and was certain of its powers. Mirror tended fire, a torch for the twins of head and heart, anamnesis in the world. A little boat journeyed over the wave of my breast. Out of its bows came the sound of someone singing. Out of its bows came the song of someone keeping time. Everything comes to the sea gate, everything with a promise to keep.

But the spirals that travel up and down in the blue are crashed. In the capitals of my mother's hand *LOVELY* gives way to *LONELY* as she loses ground to what should have been only grief. I chose poetry because every line set out so hopefully from a new margin, and because my heart was hot and unbowed. Now I am cast up on the white sand at noon with the weight of the sky on my head. I have forgotten the shape of presence in absence, of signs in wonders. Letters migrate like cells and I am writing poverty. At the iris gate I leave the world above for the world below. Lay me out in your heart for mine is lost. My head is bent down and the old journeys are broken.

4

Where did we get to? There was a hot sweet time (and tears and thunder) then marrying. The jasmine showers down, the star jasmine in its rich drifts, impossible to say how long or where next. My dress was the sky looking east over a harbour at sunset, indigo reaching for rose, all my days sheer pearl in the height before darkness. There was sojourning here a first time, sojourning here a second, one moment, for ever. There is never leaving and leaving all the time.

It's nightfall. On the waterfront the folks are throwing shoes and rice, big reception for the moon coming up, little black dog dancing and music in the air like water near the mark. Everything is served in a *jus,* nectar and all the games to be played. The car pulls up with its tin cans, there's some hooting and carrying on, the big acceleration then well-wishers drift back to the party on the beach.

We push and we pull and the shapes of the world are accommodated. Next morning there's a spring to renew the zonule in. Roses swing, dog barks. If touch is a torch and the difference still you, can it matter so very much if I do not see your face? I hold you, I kiss you. How can I go on without you? The price of the gate is too high, it tears me apart and I am afraid.

5

Is it far? Phoenixes flame on the rim of the sky. I see them everywhere proclaiming crowns that whirl overhead, crowns with the tails of comets burning. Dew falls into the valleys, into the bowls of air. Dew falls out of the air remembering fiery crests.

I have swum the vitreous distance that determines past and future, what is to come and what has been. *Take me to the river.* The sight of my eyes does not fail me here. *Throw me in the water.* Fire burns up on the rim of the sky. Dew collects below.

She lay dying in the summer house, in her own house but changed. There was a mirror left incautiously and she cried out at the changes. What have I come to, she asked, Where am I going? But she did not seem afraid. There was care of the body becoming helpless. There was return of the care given long ago to the newly born. Life and dying stood in the house together, and there was laughter as well as sorrow. The future was told washing delicate things by hand, making the room fresh, watching through the dark hours. The body fought its extinction, casting off peripheries so the heart might beat and the breath be caught. The time came when she could not see, then the time when she could not hear. Still the water was dripped in, because the throat was open, because the breath demanded, because the heart beat fiercely.

The winds of The Child battered the house where she lay. Out of a cupboard came the pink and white sheets, patched now but affording light sleep to the sleepless, folding nights and days in a consequence. So much waiting, so much to do.

6

Does it hurt? The moon rose *macula lutea*, swinging above the harbour, drawing all eyes. Every time you think you're done, round it comes again. We sat on the hillside and the moon beat a path to our feet. The boats coming home were riding lights and sail noise until they crossed the moon's path. Then there was moonlight through spinnakers and shadows that made wings on the sea. The starboard lights were jewels, the fleet came home across the path of the moon and was a wonder in our eyes.

There was morphine ready but no pain was admitted even when our questions went unanswered. She was far away and the throat was closing at last. What could we do but wait? What could we do but talk out the wait with living voices? One morning she heard us and smiled. She couldn't speak, she couldn't see but she was there, come back for the last time. We talked to her with the signal of the smile all that day. We put music in the room. We filled it with talk and were delirious with one another because of the gift of the smile. She is here, we said, she has come back.

Visual purple bleaches out in light and must be replaced in darkness. When it is replenished the dark-adapted eye can see at night. I looked out at the yellow moon and its light was a road to the city of acumen falling now to ruin in my eye. I looked over the harbour and saw the islands of vision where purples were still working at bringing night up on the screen for me. Visual purple is rhodopsin. Rhodopsin is rose sight. Dance moon, dance me to the end of love. Lift me, leave me breathless.

7

Where will it end? I hold fire and dew in the rose of my eye and something walks out hardly knowing what has been done or why. *Smoke on the water.* I want to know how it began. *Fire in the sky.* What damage under which mountain affecting whose right of return to the places where love was made. Doves whirl down behind the blue-flowering tree, sun glints up through wharf decking as I go. Doves and glints, wings in the head and still I descend. Here is the valley whose floor is too quiet, mind's dancing floor where the winds of vision convene and are wings on the sea. I am close to the centre, close to the end. I am close to where it began.

A little girl plays on a bank near the house her father built looking over the river and out to sea. The sky is blue. An old kit-bag is there full of pegs. The sun is overhead, it's late morning or early afternoon. Perhaps it is a movie. Suddenly the sky splits open. It roars, it smashes down scream for scream, nothing to be done nowhere to go, terror come home forever. She sticks her head in the old leather bag screaming. She pulls the bag over her head screaming and screaming, hooded child. The jets are cutting in over the coast on their way back to the airbase but no future explains the dark rule, ear-splitting and terrifying and now. She in the dark perhaps four years old and the future does not exist, screaming and screaming and screaming.

what happened?
my mother came
another?
my mother

rain

a meteor fell from the southern sky | when I left that land |
troubled by the weight of a heart | in the palm of my hand. *The
story.* I have spoken the words that fall | like stars into the sea.
I have been fire on the mountain | and snow on a burning tree.
The story is. A pool and a garden divided the dream | as halves of
a perfect square. In the height before darkness everything sang.
I turned and found you there. *The story is beginning.* The song of
the halves is a dark red rose | turned to the morning sun. The
night is black that cannot bind | two hearts in one. *The story is
beginning again.*

The story is a crescent, two arms and a beating hinge,
murderous changeable blade. *Weight of a heart.* The docent says
there will be no more stories because the tellers have taken them
back. *Stars into the sea.* I who ooze blood am torn and lost. I who
poke sticks in my ears listen to her telling nothing to tell. *A garden
divided.* When she is finished nothing quarters itself in my head.
Dark red.

This is the story. It is five times the mass of the sun. It is
nothing.

my face is black with crying. I walk in the mountains, I wait at the edge of the forest, I cry over the water. On my back is a cedar basket, inside it a child with frightened eyes wondering if I am hungry. It is winter. It is spring. I have the mouth of a cave and the throat of a loon. I could eat the child. My eyes stare and do not close. My face is black with crying.

I run and hunt, I caw and howl. My red parts glisten. My black mouths search. Salmonberry is one sound, thimbleberry another. Stink currant thickets my tongue. I am sleepless with anger, bitten with hate. Chisels have run to have their say in me. *Black for her darkness, red for her pain, white for her hour of vision.*

Whose eyes are those? I am looking for the house of the winter feast. If I find it there will be steaming food for my emptiness and a warm place to lie down. I will lay aside the basket and sleep. Maybe the child will creep out and run away. Or maybe I will need her small weight a while yet.

My hands are claws. I gouge. I run. I cry.

sing Andromeda. You are a mountain above a river of ice. You are
the ship for whom the mountain is named, anterior flight of sails.
You are stars standing together in somebody's alphabet, a galaxy a
green plant a girl on a rock in a hard place. Andromeda you are my
fading hope. I stand on the slow river waiting to hear you sing.

    I had courage enough when I turned and left that place. But a
horse with wings is dragging you around by the hair. *The horse was
once a garden set at the spring horizon.* Katabatic winds pour off
your glittering shoulder. Clouds sail into my eyes. *Its heart was
that Great Square which turned over when the winged horse
stumbled.* Why does the girl write silver and starlight and singing?
Because the garden of the heart is perfect. Why are heroes tall and
blue and golden? *It doesn't matter if the horse is upside down.* The
alpha star of his shoulder looks up at the alpha star of your head
inclining behind the mountain. Without you the horse of poetry
would fall right out of the sky. Without you there is no garden.
Your lucid head holds up the north corner of paradise.

    A spring horizon, an hour of vision, moving ice. Pain. Anger.
Removal. Blindness :

ice

snow feathers down gentle gentle injurious whispers *sleep and forget* kiss kiss and the roof of the world collapses compacted whispers *forget* the icecave with its jewelled snake, hiss of blades on the frozen lake, ridge of the six glaciers rehearsing the shouts of dancers *forget* revelry stillness love the snow walk where I heard train call mountain from mountain working up and down the spirals in the high passes. My hands curled in their pockets, dead obedient daughters, sleepers under the river, sleepers under the lake.

I took off my jewellery and gave it to a stranger in a tea-house saying *Bow Lake holds the tears I couldn't keep; Bow River is my voice above sorrow.* The silver blackened as it cooled against the snow and disappeared perhaps not forever. I could hear it between footfalls in the stranger's bag as he started back along the lake. It was the sound of running water. It was light honey on the wind below the pass. *Listen for my voice. Touch my wet face.* Bring me where panic has gone out of the world.

stone

I was hung on a hook three days and three nights, a corpse among corpses in the palace of disaster. I saw nothing, heard nothing, was nothing. Only this : through the lid of one eye a small song, crept under the doors of stone, capers before her who was me. Now there are two singing who lift the heavy lids of her eyes which are mine. Closer they come to the lady unloved in her hours of pain as she walking above was ever attended by joy. They stroke her temples, touch her ears, take her hands and ride with her over the jagged plain. There is blood in the bed and soon a child's head crowning between her legs.

As she who is me allows herself to be touched by their couvade, a spring begins in the rock. When she who was me asks what gift can be made for their gift they ask for the body on the wall. She looks at it, white flowers opening head to foot, and gives her assent. Quickly the strangers remove their effigy and carry it away, calling the stations of the journey as they go. Oils and tears complete the work and when they reach the surface there is no cortège, only a child crying in the night and one who brings comfort to it.

You brought me here, I (a stranger) sang the release of sorrows borne from one depth to another height. We came out of the dark loving.

that night that morning
that afternoon
the world of water
heaven's smile
the book of tears

walking in the rose-garden we have imagined the genius of a
later time. *Blessings* the temperature of body heat fall in big
drops on bare skin. The sun the wind the rain the snap of the
bow on the trail of a scent. Three ways the vista is mountains,
and terraces the colour of stars whose names are recorded on
the other side of this page. There we find ourselves one day in
early spring setting out to look for the rivers of heaven. The
journey will be described again but this small book, tattered
and begging more questions than it answers, is originary. It is
for you, your drumskin heart in need of no translation, you at
this rendezvous older but never forgotten, and the book is
what happened along the way.

Water falls in endless strings, glossy calypso files washing
off salt. Here is a comb. Here is an open window. The silver
mirror is nothing to me now though once I held it dear. You
who knock on the yellow door, sit down at my table and read.
I am going out. Eat when you are hungry, sleep when your
eyes grow heavy. The house is yours.

I was bee-belly setting out from the island of the first morning, banners streaming, delphic sons on hand. Four directions were in my company, and the bowmen of Zenith and Nadir. Everywhere we went I made songs to be fired into the hearts of strangers. Gold dust and ivory were part of the return but mostly the arrows brought back good fortune. Nothing more is needed to prove us out of the world.

Then I lost the blue-flowered tree and learned bitterness and not-bitterness though not in that order. The sky was full of triangles and peacocks tumbling fish a water snake and a table mountain. I was insensible and there were no songs, only fire-edged letters scrolling off a silent face. My arrows flamed against the abyss and were extinguished.

woodsmoke wintersweet winter-spring breakfast, a north-facing balcony looking over the archipelago. One of the sugarloaves was mine or a road by night across the southern ocean. East and west I saw it again: far slopes of afternoon, lee shoulder against the wind, atmospheric of the other's vision. All in silence.

It was gone and the chase boats useless though I knew where to go and we were quick getting off. Coming back the water was alive with seabirds hunting, feathers and fuss in a circle. Whipped up deep. I slept again in the upstairs room and this time the coast was clear. I am learning to walk in a circle.

second person so recently singular, the first step is half a world and instruments of the sky to measure. *Antlia, Apus, Ara.* You pump me up. *Carina, Circinus, Caelum.* Breastbone of the boat Delirious Moment. *Indus, Lupus, Mensa.* My indian my wolf we have made an altar. *Musca, Norma, Octans.* She, whisper. Invoking an inconspicuous quadrant we located her house. *Pyxis, Puppis, Pictor.* Stern mariner how will you compass me? I am picking up the pieces of this body and putting them in a box. *Tucana, Vela, Volans.* Somebody's alphabet painted on a globe. Flying boat. Catalina over Ramphastos. Heroes of enlightenment velivoli, books on their knees, looking up agape. *Ploomp!* Fell into what? put a finger where?

Microscopium, Telescopium, Horologium. The clock between the rivers has hourly words with a lion on the ground and a dory fish. The carpenter's square triangulates views from the top deck where I wanted to remain indefinitely, musing on the sculptor's tools, the painter's edge, Sophy's zoo. Phoenix meets Columba and they both go up in smoke. These notes on my knee. This hiatus.

At the ticket office my documentation was examined. *Are you blind?* the fuller's boy asked. He was in charge of the fare. *Yes* I said *I am.* In the change was a small silver leaf.

crossing quay crossing customs the end is here *that's it! no more! you can all go home!* M. Dumnov in a sandwich board shouting to ants on the Novotel wall the day government fell in the city of light. He was ignored. There were flags on every corner, bread and wine and lilies in broad cups, and plaques commemorating other sunny days at the top of the elevator well. The crowds surged after their boat. Doves flew over the city. Every step was a return without memory to a place of origin. *narcissi. baked chocolate.* Helium in the hands of children. Suds in the fountain.

There is a manner of people called Corybantes who believe when the moon is in eclipse that it is enchanted and therefore they beat their basins with thick strokes to release her. Their worship is performed with noisy and extravagant rites. They howl it out, dancing and glowing on the high tops with frantic fire. A procession is made and numinous images carried but the hour of conjunction is not revealed. It is said the celebrants sleep with their eyes open.

We went anonymous in the din, found students sitting on the ground with scripts beating their hands and saying nothing. In their eyes I saw the ring on my finger begin a clockwise turn. In their faces were our faces all dewy at the centre of the world.

pyrophoric and breathing sharply at the incline we enter a narrow passage where torches flare. Such incantation, such prière! Wild cries and the frenzied music of flutes drums and cymbals *I always order this I'm always on my mobile I've got five dollars to last the weekend.* Street clowns, sad parrots, luting mummers *I'd like a bed on the Twentieth Century please.* Doppling knots of lingua in our ears, the speed of red light expanded.

Further up the lane is what we're looking for, sparks and hammering, an artisan at his trade under the old volcano. Our pageant winds alongside his booth fingering the silverware on its velvet, trying on bits of magic armour, haggling with the girl assistant. Her limping boss is almost finished with the piece, light strong alloy, numbers for a flamey pin. The price is paid *léger léger* and we're on our way across the Place de la Guerre with its shells and fruit stall. Apples on the bough. Fish in the sea. She, whisper goddess, blew.

An afternoon flight. Hot rain. *I spent months getting that right.* A row of numbers, a row of letters, a row of lights. Moon chew. Stipule. Fire. Confusion rejoins history by the Courthouse being preserved to face an uncertain future. Above us more steps set into the mountainside. Cottonwood snow.

risers

blossom

oxyphoric

flight of sails

other places

indigo

overflowing

almond

money pool

roman fleuve

one moment

so fearful

summer house

storms of noise

old motors

hesperidium

dark-adapted

swim out

momentum

occident

long talk

light honey

atmospheric

barefoot

o phoeb

I hunted you down in the grasses of summer and we fought on the river bank for the last word, an interrogative curve that would not yield or cease. *For she too sailing overhead* there is no last word, as there is no other way but to come through this trench. To walk at sunset *on clear nights* near the great river come by the same divide to where we are. A broken circle *in the likeness of* palmettos and into it our corybantes banging on a drum, emancipation in the park, whoops and yells *the silver moon* and a speech about the road ahead. *Looked down with pleasure on* a lady with bird wings kneeling in front of a king *her own calm image.* If it's too high you know it will hurt your feet. If it's a dream it is already *reflected* time and mind *on the calm.*

A mock cortège rounds the fountain, climbing the shallow steps. When it reaches the grove there are greetings and a mingling of process. Everything hangs in the balance. The pedestal is empty, the casket sprung, there is a throng and a clearing *the burnished surface* where I step forward as if for the first time. There is enough light, deep breath *of the lake, her mirror* to read by. Quiet flick of pages. Lip lap shiver. When I lift my eyes from the last words you are there. Together we make morning.

if this float would take my weight
and the words be made of air again